Paper New York
Build Your Own Big Apple

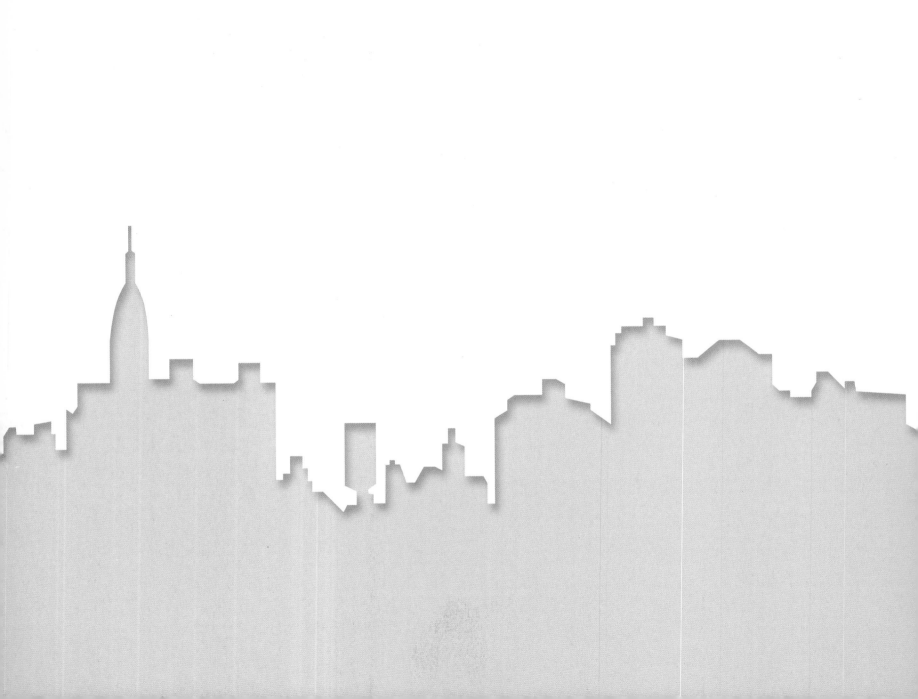

Paper New York
Build Your Own Big Apple

Kell Black

Universe

First published in the United States of America in 2010 by
UNIVERSE PUBLISHING
A Division of Rizzoli International Publications, Inc.
300 Park Avenue South
New York, NY 10010
www.rizzoliusa.com

This book was created by
Ivy Press
210 High Street, Lewes
East Sussex BN7 2NS, UK
www.ivy-group.co.uk

Copyright © Ivy Press Limited 2010

Library of Congress Cataloging-in-Publication Data

Black, Kell.
  Paper New York : build your own Big Apple / Kell Black.
    p. cm.
  ISBN 978-0-7893-2079-7 (pbk.)
  1. Paper work. 2. Architectural models--New York (State)--New York.
  3. New York (N.Y.)--Buildings, structures, etc. I. Title.
  TT870.B538 2010
  736'.98--dc22
                        2010018847

2010 2011 2012 2013 / 10 9 8 7 6 5 4 3 2 1

ISBN: 978-0-7893-2079-7

This book was conceived, designed, and produced by
Ivy Press
CREATIVE DIRECTOR Peter Bridgewater
PUBLISHER Jason Hook
EDITORIAL DIRECTOR Tom Kitch
SENIOR DESIGNER Kate Haynes
DESIGNER Glyn Bridgewater
PHOTOGRAPHER Andrew Perris
ILLUSTRATOR Kell Black
MAP ILLUSTRATOR Richard Palmer
PICTURE RESEARCHER Katie Greenwood

Printed in China

Color origination by Ivy Press Reprographics

Dedicated to Anne

Contents

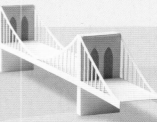

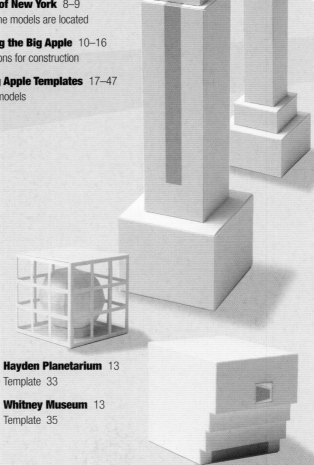

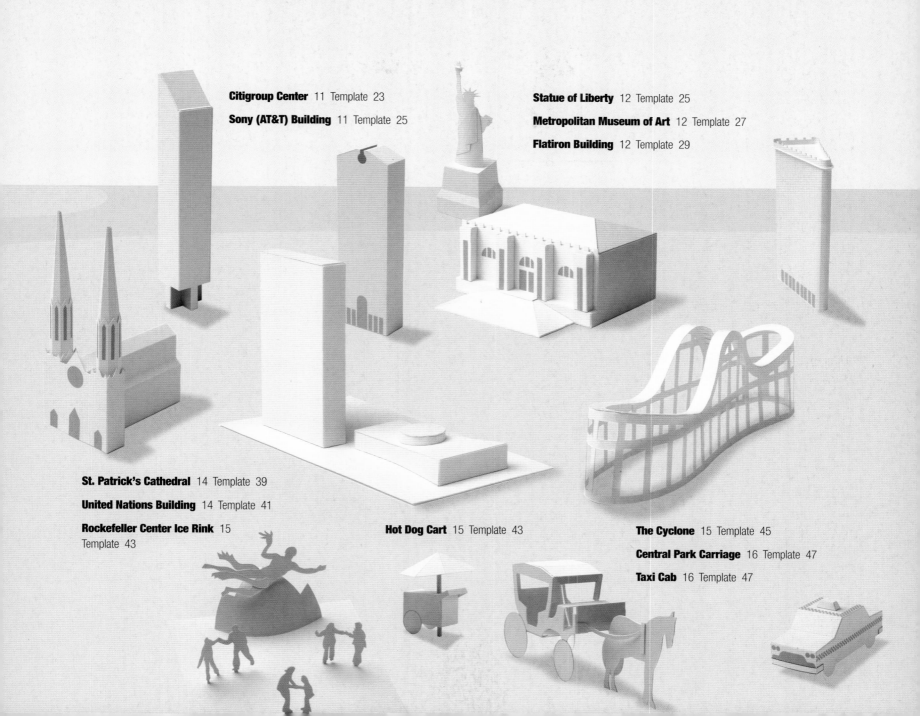

At a time when over half of us are living in cities for the first time in history, New York symbolizes the ultimate urban existence. Over eight million people, speaking more than 150 distinct languages, interact in an area of just 305 square miles, making it little wonder that the city is famed for its collective insomnia.

A visit to New York is a study in contrasts. There is the ground-level hustle and bustle of the city's streets versus the stately tranquility of its architecture, one at the human scale, the other at a size that sometimes defies comprehension.

I often arrive in New York via the Metro North Railway at Grand Central Station. After a short walk along the dimly lit train platform, you step into the terminal itself. Hundreds of travelers are always rushing to and from trains while above you floats the station's enormous blue ceiling with its famous twinkling constellations. Welcome to New York!

The models in this book seek to capture both the big and small experiences of the Big Apple, from the brief encounter with a hot dog vendor to the enormous span of the Brooklyn Bridge.

The average guidebook to New York City runs well over two hundred pages, so there is no lack of interesting subjects to re-create. How, then, were the models chosen? I tried to strike a balance between personal favorites—the Sony (AT&T) Building and the Whitney Museum, for example—and the city's "greatest hits," such as the Empire State Building and the Guggenheim Museum. Fortunately, most models fell into both camps.

Many of the models are of buildings, but some experiences were best described in nonarchitectural terms, such as the ice rink and the hot dog cart. In all instances, the intention was not to design scale models, but rather to create paper sculptures that captured the essence of a building or a scene.

Everything in this book can be made with simple household materials—a craft knife, a straightedge, white glue, tweezers, and toothpicks—and without any prior paper modeling experience. Simply follow the instructions, take your time, and enjoy the process.

You will need only a few simple tools to help you assemble all the models in the book. They are: white glue, such as Elmer's; toothpicks for applying the glue neatly; a pair of tweezers to help you hold things in place; a round pencil or a dowel for rounding out curved sections; a straightedge or ruler; a pin; and a butter knife or a ballpoint pen that no longer writes. (The last items are used to score the pieces before folding.) You may also find it useful to have an emery board and a sharp craft knife or scalpel on hand.

Paper modeling is not difficult, but it does require patience and cleanliness. Find yourself a well-lit work space free from clutter, and always follow this order: look, read, detach, fold, glue.

Begin each model by looking at the template and any accompanying diagrams. Be sure also to inspect the photo of the finished piece, above the instructions. Read the instructions carefully and remove the die-cut pieces from the page, keeping them in numerical order. Some of the pieces may have tiny tufts as a result of die-cutting. You may easily sand these away with a few light strokes of the emery board.

Score the pieces before folding them. Do this with a butter knife or a ballpoint pen that you're absolutely sure has run out of ink. With your straightedge as a guide, run the knife or pen over the solid gray fold lines. This compresses the paper's fibers so that it creases neatly away from you.

Note: There are a few dashed lines that need to be folded from the opposite side into a valley fold (see the illustration on this page). To do this, poke a tiny hole with a pin at the extremities of each dashed line, then turn the piece over. Using the two holes as guides, line up the straightedge and score from hole to hole. Now the piece will fold cleanly toward you.

Further detail may be added to some of the projects such as the Brooklyn Bridge and the Statue of Liberty by cutting out the dark gray shapes (negative spaces) where instructed (see the illustration on this page). Use a sharp craft knife or scalpel and a metal straightedge for this. With the straightedge as a guide and brace, gently but firmly cut away the gray shapes. Use caution so that you cut only the paper and not yourself!

As for gluing, less is more. In the words of my first-grade teacher: "One dot glues a lot." You can keep things neat by squirting out a small amount of glue onto a scrap piece of cardboard. Then use a toothpick to apply the glue to the shaded areas of the tabs.

Finally, take your time. Building the models is half the fun, so work slowly and thoughtfully. Test fit the pieces before gluing, and hold each assembly for a slow count of twenty to let the glue set before moving on to the next step.

Enjoy.

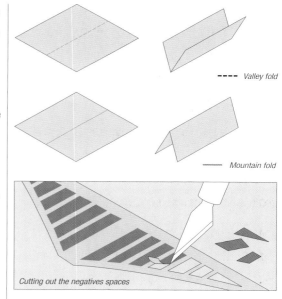

---- *Valley fold*

—— *Mountain fold*

Cutting out the negatives spaces

Paper New York features the city's most iconic structures and showcases the vast range of styles—from art deco to postmodernism—that have influenced its architects over time. All of the structures are located in Manhattan, with the exception of the Cyclone, which is to the south, in Coney Island.

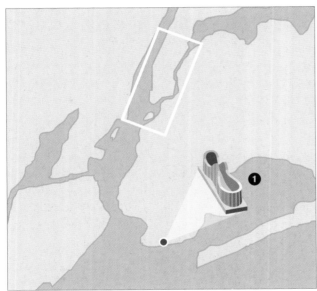

❶ The Cyclone
834 Surf Avenue
Completed 1927
Architect Vernon Keenan

❷ Statue of Liberty
Liberty Island
Completed 1886
Architect Frédéric Bartholdi

❸ Woolworth Building
233 Broadway at Barclay Street
Completed 1913
Architect Cass Gilbert

❹ Brooklyn Bridge
Completed 1883
Architects John Augustus Roebling

❺ Flatiron Building
175 5th Avenue at 23rd Street
Completed 1902
Architect Daniel Burnham

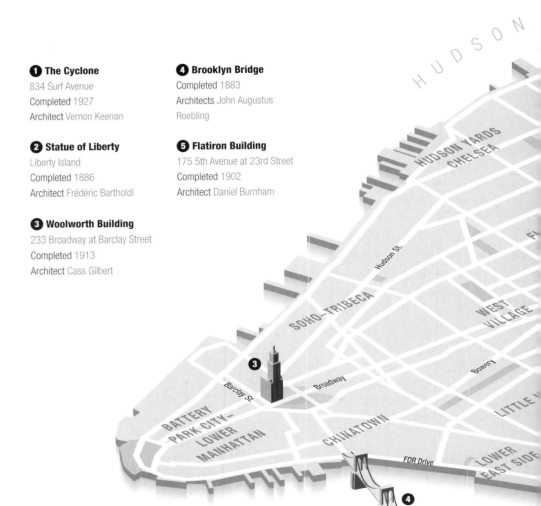

A Map of New York

13 Hayden Planetarium
Central Park West at 79th Street
Completed 2000
Architect James Stewart
Polshek

**14 Metropolitan
Museum of Art**
1000 5th Avenue at 82nd Street
Completed 1959
Architects Calvert Vaux
and Jacob Wrey Mould

15 Whitney Museum
945 Madison Avenue
at 75th Street
Completed 1966
Architects Marcel Breuer
and Hamilton Smith

16 Guggenheim Museum
1071 5th Avenue at 89th Street
Completed 1959
Architect Frank Lloyd Wright

10 United Nations Building
760 United Nations Plaza
Completed 1950
Architects Wallace Harrison,
Max Abramovitz, and
Le Corbusier

11 Sony (AT&T) Building
550 Madison Avenue
at 56th Street
Completed 1984
Architect Philip Johnson

12 Citigroup Center
601 Lexington Avenue
at 53rd Street
Completed 1978
Architect Hugh Stubbins

8 Chrysler Building
405 Lexington Avenue
at 42nd Street
Completed 1930
Architect William van Alen

9 St. Patrick's Cathedral
460 Madison Avenue
at 50th Street
Completed 1879
Architect James Renwick, Jr.

6 Empire State Building
350 5th Avenue at 34th Street
Completed 1931
Architects Richmond Shreve,
William Lamb, and
Arthur Harmon

**7 Rockefeller
Center Ice Rink**
5th Avenue at 50th Street
Completed 1936
Architect Raymond Hood

Empire State Building

No collection of iconic buildings of New York would be complete without the Empire State Building, the signature building of the city. It was designed by William F. Lamb of the Shreve, Lamb, and Harmon architectural partnership. The design was based on the drawings for a similar but smaller structure, the twenty-one-story Reynolds Building in Winston-Salem, North Carolina. The Empire State Building is the tallest building in New York, and it is also the third tallest building in North America.

■ Begin by assembling the main section of the building, *Empire 1*.

■ Assemble *Empire 2*. When dry, attach to *Empire 1*.

■ Build the base, *Empire 3*, making sure to leave the bottom flap (without the square guide) open for now.

■ Build the spire, *Empire 4*, by gluing the two pieces spine to spine. To do this, first fold the two sections in half so that each piece is at a right angle, then use a toothpick to apply a thin line of glue along the spine of one piece. With the two pieces folded closed, glue one to the spine of the other. Let dry.

■ Attach the main section to the base. Glue the bottom flap closed.

■ With a tiny line of glue along the base of the spire (*Empire 4*), position it gently onto the top of *Empire 2*. Keep an eye out for King Kong, Fay Wray, and the biplanes.

Chrysler Building

The Chrysler Building is a masterpiece of art deco architecture. When it was completed in 1930, it was the tallest building in the world. The Empire State Building surpassed it in 1931.

■ Begin by constructing the main body of the building, *Chrysler 1*.

■ While this dries, assemble *Chrysler 2*, *3*, and *4*, which make up the distinctive art deco tower—they will nestle inside each other like Russian dolls. Glue the outermost piece, *Chrysler 4*, to the top of *Chrysler 1*, by applying a thin bead of glue along *Chrysler 4*'s bottom edge and positioning it in place along the outermost glue guidelines.

■ Follow suit with *Chrysler 3* and *2*.

■ The pinnacle comprises two pieces glued spine to spine, *Chrysler 5*. Simply fold the two pieces in half, then use a toothpick to apply a thin bead of glue along the spine of one piece. With the two pieces folded closed, glue one to the spine of the other. When dry, put a drop of glue on the bottom and slide it into the nest of pieces already in place.

■ Assemble *Chrysler 6*. Glue *Chrysler 1* to *6*.

■ Assemble the base of the building (*Chrysler 7*), but leave the bottom flap open for the time being. This will allow you to reach in with a finger or two when gluing *Chrysler 6* to the base. When all the pieces are in place, glue the bottom flap closed, then take the elevator to the top for a stunning view of Midtown Manhattan.

Brooklyn Bridge

Designed by John Augustus Roebling, the Brooklyn Bridge became an iconic element of the city's skyline while still under construction. Most of the construction was supervised by Roebling's son and daughter-in-law, Washington and Emily Warren Roebling.

■ To build a more detailed version, where the spaces between the cables are cut out, begin here (if not, move on to the next step). Using a sharp craft knife and a metal straightedge (to steady the blade), cut out the pieces between the cables on *Brooklyn 3* and *4*.

■ Assemble the distinctive piers of the bridge, *Brooklyn 1* and *2*. Glue the rectangular tabs to those with the diagonal corners.

■ Glue *Brooklyn 1* and *2* to the inside of *Brooklyn 3*, the first of the two spans. Align the tops of the piers with the top edge of the spans.

■ Glue the roadway into place. Begin with *Brooklyn 5*. Fold down the tabs and glue to the inside of *Brooklyn 3*. Be sure to line up the bottom of the tab with the bottom of the span. Repeat with *Brooklyn 6* and *7*.

■ Attach *Brooklyn 4* to the rest of the structure by gluing the two piers to its inside. At this point, the roadway is attached only on one side of the bridge. Push the unglued side down and slightly below the bridge to easily apply glue to the remaining tabs. Push the section back up into the bridge, lining them up as before with the bottom of the span. You may now travel from Manhattan to Brooklyn and back again.

Guggenheim Museum

The Solomon R. Guggenheim Museum is most commonly known simply as the Guggenheim. The building was Frank Lloyd Wright's last major project, and when it opened in 1959, it was a critical battleground for both proponents and detractors of modern architecture. Along with the Metropolitan Museum of Art and other institutions, the Guggenheim is a part of the city's "Museum Mile."

■ Begin by constructing the distinctive cork-shaped structure of the museum, *Guggenheim 1*. Before gluing the piece together, gently round it out by pulling it over the edge of a tabletop or by rolling it over a round pencil or a dowel. Glue and allow to dry thoroughly before proceeding.

■ Glue the roof, *Guggenheim 2*, to the top of *Guggenheim 1*. Take your time and attach only a few tabs at a time, putting a dab of glue only on the tabs you are attaching at that time. While applying pressure from within and without, hold each section for a slow count of twenty before moving on.

■ Assemble the base of the building, *Guggenheim 3*. Again, round out the four corners by rolling them over a round pencil or dowel before gluing. The four tabs are attached to the insides of their corresponding mates. Do not glue the very bottom closed yet.

■ Now attach the previously completed section, *Guggenheim 1* and *2*, to *Guggenheim 3*. When dry, glue the bottom closed. Take a wander around and enjoy the latest exhibition of contemporary art.

Citigroup Center

Featuring a roof dramatically set at a 45-degree angle, the Citigroup Center is one of the most distinctive profiles on the New York skyline. The building's base is nearly as impressive as its top: The fifty-nine-story structure appears to stand on four stilts. The building was designed by Hugh Stubbins, Jr., and was the first building in the United States to feature a tuned mass damper, a 400-ton stabilizer that counteracts sway caused by wind. Opened in 1977, it is one of a dozen buildings in the States that uses double-decker elevators that service odd and even floors.

■ This model consists of only one piece, but its lower section contains a series of valley and mountain folds, giving the building its distinctive indented look. In short, the four edges of the base push in on themselves to create a plus-sign-shaped pedestal. (See the detailed illustration next to the template.)

■ As always, score all folds before gluing, making sure to follow the rules for valley folds as outlined in the general instructions. The four indentations may be folded in as you glue the sides of the building together, or you may wait until the entire building is built and then gently push them in at the end with the aid of tweezers. When you've finished, marvel at the engineering ingenuity as you enter the building.

Sony (AT&T) Building

Philip Johnson's postmodern masterpiece opened in 1984 amid much controversy. Mocked by some as an enormous Chippendale highboy due to its highly ornamental pediment, the building was applauded by others who saw in it a move away from modernism's stark glass and chrome aesthetic. Whatever your opinion, the thirty-seven-story building in Midtown Manhattan cannot be overlooked. It is interesting to note that this postmodern icon was designed by the same architect who helped bring the modernist International Style of architecture to the United States in the late 1920s and 1930s.

■ This building consists of only one piece. First attach the sides, then the bottom and finally the top. The roof's large rectangles are glued to their corresponding tabs, but the smaller sections are simply folded over and adhered with just the slightest touch of glue. Stand back and admire Philip Johnson's postmodern masterpiece.

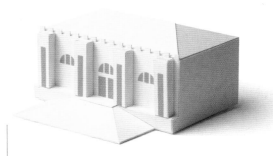

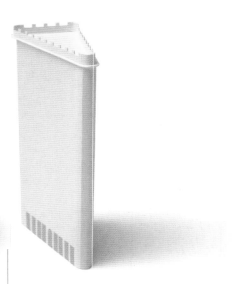

Statue of Liberty

Officially titled "The Statue of Liberty Enlightening the World," Frédéric Batholdi's sculpture was dedicated on October 28, 1886. Lady Liberty stands in New York Harbor, and for generations of immigrants it was the first glimpse of their new home.

■ Begin with the body of Lady Liberty herself, *Liberty 1*. Using a sharp craft knife and a metal straightedge (to steady the blade), cut out the pieces between the spikes on the crown. To give her greater dimension, slightly curve out the piece lengthwise by rolling it gently over a dowel or round pencil. A subtle curve is all that is needed. Make sure to fold and glue her left hand in place on the tablet she's holding.

■ Slightly round out pieces *Liberty 2* and *3*. Glue the pieces one on top of the other to give her toga dimension. Don't forget to fold and glue the small triangular section on *Liberty 2*.

■ Construct the base, *Liberty 4*. Observe the dashed line that indicates a valley fold. Mark, score, and fold as indicated in the general instructions.

■ Apply a thin bead of glue to the bottom of *Liberty 1* and gently place on the base. Hold for a count of twenty so that the glue sets.

■ Place a tiny dot of glue on either side of the torch and attach *Liberty 5* over the flame. When it's complete, take a trip to the observation decks in either Lady Liberty's crown or torch to take in the spectacular view of Lower Manhattan.

Metropolitan Museum of Art

Affectionately called "The Met," the museum stands on the eastern edge of Central Park. Founded in 1870, the central stone building was designed by architects Calvert Vaux and Jacob Wrey Mould, but over the years the museum has grown to more than twenty times its original size; it now consists of more than twenty-five buildings. The spectacular stairway leading to the main entrance is a favorite meeting spot for visitors and New Yorkers.

■ Begin by folding the facade, *Met 1*, as indicated on the template. Don't overlook the dashed valley fold.

■ Attach *Met 1* to the bulk of the building, *Met 2*. Fold and glue the four columns, *Met 3*, together. Set aside and let dry.

■ Attach the roof, *Met 4*, to the building, ensuring that you glue the gray tab at the front of the roof to the back of the crenellated facade.

■ Attach the columns to the front of the building. Fold and glue the stairs, *Met 5*, to the building. Attach the completed building to the base, *Met 6*. When visiting the Met, be sure to look for Michelangelo's *The Study for the Libyan Sibyl*, one of the finest drawings to be held in a museum in America.

Flatiron Building

Daniel Burnham's 1902 skyscraper has come to be known by its nickname, Flatiron, because it so closely resembled the shape of a cast clothing iron. In fact, the whole neighborhood surrounding the building is now known as the Flatiron District.

■ Begin with *Flatiron 1*. The corners of the building are rounded, so it is essential that you round out the corners before gluing the structure together. Do this by rolling the three corners over a small dowel or round pencil. (Light gray vertical lines designate the corners.) Once rounded, glue the piece together.

■ *Flatiron 2* provides support and structure for the base of the model. Fold the three flaps down and slide the section up and into *Flatiron 1* so that the tabs are flush with the lowest edge of the building.

■ *Flatiron 3* provides additional structure to the model. Fold the three flaps down and glue to the inside top of *Flatiron 1*. The top of *Flatiron 3* should be flush with the top edge of *Flatiron 1*.

■ *Flatiron 4* is the decorative roof of the building. Attach it to *Flatiron 3* so that it overhangs equally on all three sides.

■ *Flatiron 5* is the crenellated parapet. Round its corners as above, then fold the tabs underneath. Glue the ends of *Flatiron 5* together, then glue it to the light gray outline on *Flatiron 4*. Your building is now the centerpiece of the Flatiron District.

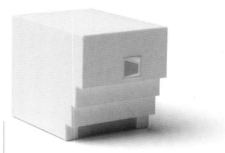

MTA Subway Car

"New York, New York, what a wonderful town. People ride in a hole in the ground!" The New York subway system is one of the oldest and most extensive mass transportation systems in the world. The subway portion opened in 1904 and is one of only a handful of public transportation systems in the United States that runs twenty-four hours a day, every day of the year. Street musicians abound on the platforms, but restrooms are rare. The famed alligators that allegedly prowl the subway and sewers are just an urban legend.

■ This model consists of only two pieces but it is one of the more difficult ones. Proceed slowly and carefully and do not do this one first.

■ Score and fold all the tabs, the roof, and the end sections of *Subway 1*. Glue the long side wall of the car to the two ends, making sure that the roof tabs are inside. When dry, you may glue the roof tabs to the inside of the ends by applying glue with a toothpick and then using the tweezers to hold the tabs firmly in place. Take your time. When the roof and ends are dry, attach the bottom flap. It is not necessary to put glue on the three triangular tabs at either end.

■ Fold and glue the wheel assembly, *Subway 2*, together. When dry, glue to the bottom of the subway car. When you're ready to take a ride, double check to make sure that you're getting on a local and not an express—you don't want to miss your stop.

Hayden Planetarium

The distinctive architecture of the Rose Center for Earth and Space, which houses the Hayden Planetarium, was designed by James Polshek and opened in 2000, replacing the original 1935 structure. The new planetarium opened amid much controversy because of its redesigned solar system exhibition, which featured only eight planets; Pluto was excluded due to its redesignation as a minor planet. The planetarium is especially popular with children and received over a thousand visitors an hour when it first opened.

■ Assemble each half of the sphere, *Hayden 1* and *2*. Let each half dry completely before creating the final sphere.

■ Assemble the large cube that makes up the Rose Center, *Hayden 3* and *4*. *Hayden 3* contains the roof; keep the rooftop open.

■ Glue the two halves of the sphere together. Reach a finger inside to apply pressure from within and without while gluing. When dry, assemble the sphere's base, *Hayden 5*, and attach it to the bottom of the sphere. Attach the assembled sphere to the inside of the cube. Glue the top closed, then sit back and enjoy the latest star show—it will be the clearest sky you'll see in New York City.

Whitney Museum

The Whitney Museum of American Art is a distinctly modern building designed by architects Marcel Breuer and Hamilton P. Smith, and its exterior accurately reflects the mission of the collection to emphasize the work of living twentieth and twenty-first century artists. The museum is best known for its Biennial, an exhibition of contemporary art dubbed by some as the "show everyone loves to hate." In addition to showcasing the work of younger artists, the museum houses an extensive collection devoted to work from the first half of the twentieth century.

■ Although this model consists of only two pieces, it has more valley folds than all the other structures. Refer to the general instructions and fold the dashed-line valley folds from the back using your pin, straightedge, and scoring tool. Both pieces require this.

■ Begin by assembling the front window, *Whitney 1*. When dry, attach from behind to *Whitney 2*.

■ Assemble *Whitney 2*, making sure to leave the bottom of the building open until the last step so that you can reach in to secure the facade to its tabs. When dry, enter the museum and visit the Biennial. It's always controversial.

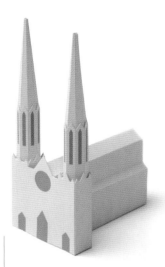

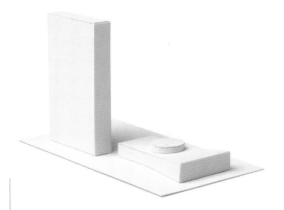

Woolworth Building

This neo-Gothic fifty-seven-story skyscraper was designed by architect Cass Gilbert. Since its opening in 1913, it has remained one of the tallest buildings in New York. The whole building is a gem, but the tower is its centerpiece. Scaled so that it can be clearly read from street level, the tower is both massive and elegant, climbing squarely from its base to its distinctive pyramid top. With its strong allusions to European Gothic churches, the building was dubbed the "Cathedral of Commerce" at its dedication.

■ It is best to build this model of the tower from the Woolworth Building from the bottom up, in numerical order (*Woolworth 1–4*). This is a straightforward model—the only detail you must be sure to observe is the dashed lines (valley folds) on *Woolworth 5* and score accordingly. (See general building notes.) These "wings" are glued back-to-back, to each other, to form decorative buttresses (see detail).

■ Using a sharp craft knife and a metal straightedge (to steady the blade), cut out the shaded areas at the top of *Woolworth 7*. This last piece fits snugly around the spire, *Woolworth 6*, like a necklace. Enjoy the splendor of this nearly one hundred-year-old building, one of the world's original skyscrapers.

St. Patrick's Cathedral

St. Patrick's Cathedral stands in central Manhattan across from Rockefeller Center. The neo-Gothic building was designed by James Renwick, Jr. Construction began in 1858, was interrupted during the Civil War, and was completed in 1878. The cathedral was dedicated in May 1879 by John McCloskey, America's first cardinal. At the time of its construction, citizens worried that the building's lot was too remote from the city proper.

■ Begin with the facade, *St. Patrick's 1*. Fold the ends, as indicated in the diagram, to create the two towers. Fold the platforms at the tops of the towers and glue them into place, then glue sides A and B to the back of the facade. Set aside.

■ Assemble *St. Patrick's 2*. Attach piece *1* to *2*, as indicated in the detailed drawing.

■ Fold and glue *St. Patrick's 3* and *4* to create octagonal towers.

■ Fold and glue *St. Patrick's 5* and *6* to create their cones. Apply glue to the tabs of *St. Patrick's 5* and slide up and into *St. Patrick's 3*, as shown in the illustration. Stop where indicated, just before pulling the cone out of the base. Reach in with tweezers to squeeze the tabs firmly. Repeat with *St. Patrick's 4* and *6*.

■ Put a thin bead of glue on the bottom edges of *St. Patrick's 3* and *4* and gently attach them where indicated on the platforms on *St. Patrick's 1*. Amen.

United Nations Building

The United Nations headquarters is located by the East River in Manhattan, although its grounds are considered international territory. The tall central structure—the Secretariat Building—was designed by Le Corbusier and Oscar Niemeyer, and the domed General Assembly Hall was designed by an international team of eleven architects, which reflects the worldwide mission of the UN. Visitors to the UN Plaza are greeted with the 192 flags from all of the member nations, arranged alphabetically in English.

■ Assemble *United Nations 1* and adhere to base, *United Nations 2*.

■ Assemble *United Nations 3*. The roof has a slight curve to it so round it ever so slightly with a dowel or round pencil. Put aside.

■ Assemble the building's distinctive dome, *United Nations 4* and *5*. Attach this assembled section to the roof of *United Nations 3*. It is important to line up the small gray dot on the side of piece *4* with the dot on the roof of *United Nations 3* so that the roof of the dome is flat.

■ Adhere the completed building to the base. Enter the Plaza and witness the United Nations working toward international peace.

Rockefeller Center Ice Rink

Rockefeller Center is made up of nineteen buildings spread out over twenty-two acres in Midtown Manhattan, and the most popular spot for tourists and residents alike is the ice-skating rink on the lower plaza at the base of 30 Rockefeller Center. The statue of Prometheus, overlooking the rink, was designed by sculptor Paul Manship. The skating venue was opened in 1936.

■ Begin with the statue of Prometheus, *Rockefeller 1*. Using a sharp craft knife and a metal straightedge (to steady the blade), cut out the shaded areas around the flames Prometheus is holding. Fold and attach the sash, *Rockefeller 2*, to the front and back of Prometheus.

■ Slightly curve *Rockefeller 3* by rolling it gently over a round pencil or dowel. Glue the center tab to the back so that the gray semicircles form a circle. Attach Prometheus to the gray circle on the completed *Rockefeller 3*. When dry, glue the whole section to the base, *Rockefeller 4*.

■ Gently fold the three pairs of skaters, *Rockefeller 5–7*, toward you, bending them just a bit where they hold hands. With a whisper of glue on the bottom edges of their skates, attach the pairs to their corresponding marks on the rink. The mother and child are front and center, the couple is to the left, and the two sisters are to the right. After you've spent an hour on the ice, take a break, sip a cup of hot chocolate, and rest up for more figure eights.

Hot Dog Cart

The ubiquitous hot dog cart can be seen on nearly every street corner in New York, selling not only hot dogs but also gyros, kebabs, pretzels, falafels, soft drinks, and ice cream. In recent years, certain vendors have received high marks from prominent food critics in the city, and it is estimated that at least fifteen percent of all hot dogs consumed in the United States are purchased from street vendors.

■ Begin by cutting off the pointed ends of a toothpick so that it matches the length of the printed guide. This will become the umbrella's support.

■ Using a pin, poke two holes into the small circles on the top and bottom of *Cart 1* and widen them, as necessary, with a pointed toothpick so that the umbrella support passes snugly through them. Remove the toothpick and set aside.

■ Glue *Cart 1* together. Attach *Cart 2*. Slide the trimmed toothpick through the top and bottom of the cart.

■ Glue *Cart 3* together. When dry, put a drop of glue on the top of the toothpick and place *Cart 3* gently on top. Order a can of soda and a large hot dog with "the works" from your cart. Bon appetit!

The Cyclone

The Coney Island Cyclone opened to much fanfare in 1927. The wooden roller coaster was designed by Vernan Kennan, and park legend has it that in 1948, the coaster's first hair-raising drop caused a man suffering from aphonia to scream: "I feel sick!" These were his first words in decades.

■ You may build this model as is, or you may add more detail by cutting out the dark gray spaces between the coaster's girders. (See page 7 for more details.)

■ The Cyclone requires plenty of concentrated gluing; don't build this one first.

■ Begin by rounding out *Cyclone 1* and *2* to form the curved sections at each end. Glue *Cyclone 2* to *Cyclone 1*, overlapping the ends of *2* onto the light gray glue areas of *1*. Let dry. Notice the small gray dot at the top of *Cyclone 2*. This is one end of the coaster. Continue to round this end out until it forms a near semicircle. The opposite end of the coaster needs to be formed similarly. Refer to *Cyclone 3* to see how curved to make the sides. That is, gently form the base so that it generally matches the footprint of *Cyclone 3*.

■ Attach *Cyclone 3* to the base. Begin by lining up the gray dots on pieces *2* and *3*. Work slowly and carefully, gluing only a few tabs at a time. Wash your hands of excess glue when necessary. When it's dry, board the roller coaster and remember to hang on tight! The first drop is a doozy.

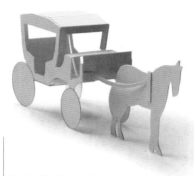

Central Park Carriage

Visitors to Central Park, designed by Frederick Law Olmstead and Calvert Vaux, can explore the grounds in a number of ways—on foot, by bicycle, via pedicab, or in a picturesque horse drawn carriage. Carriage rides began in 1935, and after the September 11, 2001 terrorist attacks, Mayor Rudolph Giuliani personally visited the horse stables to ask the cabbies to return to work in order to help restore normal life to the city.

■ A pair of tweezers is essential for making this model neatly.

■ Begin with *Carriage 1*. Using a sharp craft knife and a metal straightedge (to steady the blade), cut out the sides of the carriage. Glue the rest of the roof to the side of the carriage to which it is already partly attached. This is not as confusing as it sounds. The roof essentially wraps around the front, back, and bottom of the carriage. Slightly round the section without tabs, the small area between the back carriage window and the base.

■ Next, carefully glue the opposite side of the carriage to the roof and base. Use tweezers to reach into the carriage to hold the pieces in place while gluing. Fold the driver's seat over and glue into place.

■ Using a sharp craft knife, cut out the shaded area from the horse's harness, *Carriage 2*, then fold as indicated in the drawing. Attach it first to the back of the horse, *Carriage 3*, and then to the front of the carriage. When enjoying a romantic ride in your carriage, be sure to kiss your sweetheart when passing under one of the park's bridges.

Taxi Cab

Yellow taxis outnumber the pigeons on New York's busy streets, and for decades it was the distinctive Checker cab that people hailed when in a rush. Pulled from production in 1982, the Checker cab has been replaced by a variety of models, but the NYC cabs still retain their signature color. Hailing a cab is something of an art form, and cabs seldom stop for the timid. Be bold!

■ This is a very straightforward model consisting of only two pieces, but, as with the Central Park carriage, tweezers are necessary to build it neatly.

■ Fold the flaps and surfaces of *Cab 1* as indicated. Don't overlook the two valley folds at the base of the front and rear windshields. Glue the hood and grille to the front of the cab, then attach the ends of the bumper to the sides of the cab. Glue the trunk to the back of the cab. Again, fasten the bumper in place. Keep the bottom open for now.

■ Glue *Cab 2* as indicated. Put just a dab of glue on the bottom edges of this piece and fasten to the top of the cab. Apply slight pressure from inside the cab if necessary. Glue the bottom of the taxi closed. Jump in and take the cab downtown. Don't forget to tip the driver.

Empire State Building

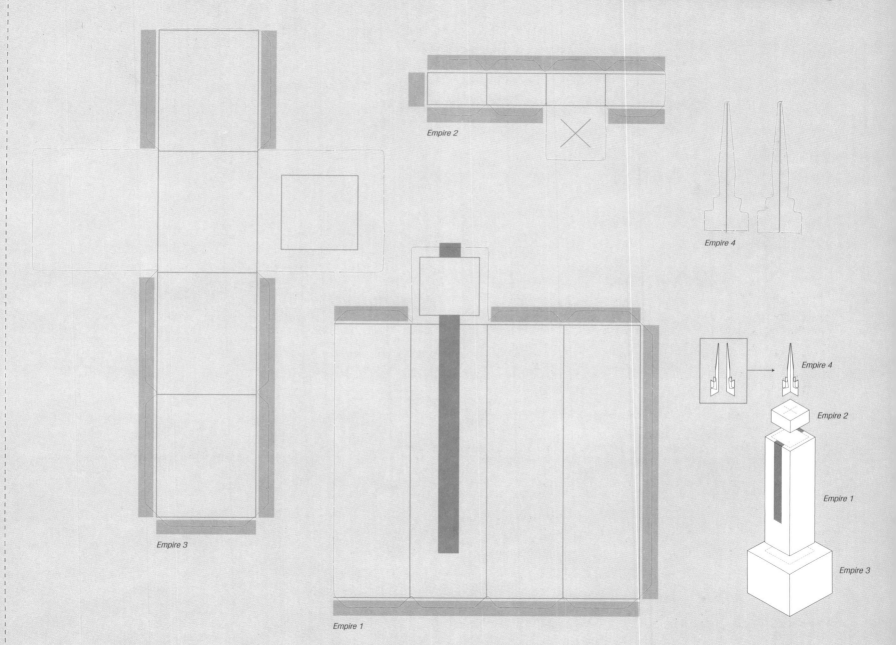

Empire 2

Empire 4

Empire 3

Empire 1

Empire 4

Empire 2

Empire 1

Empire 3

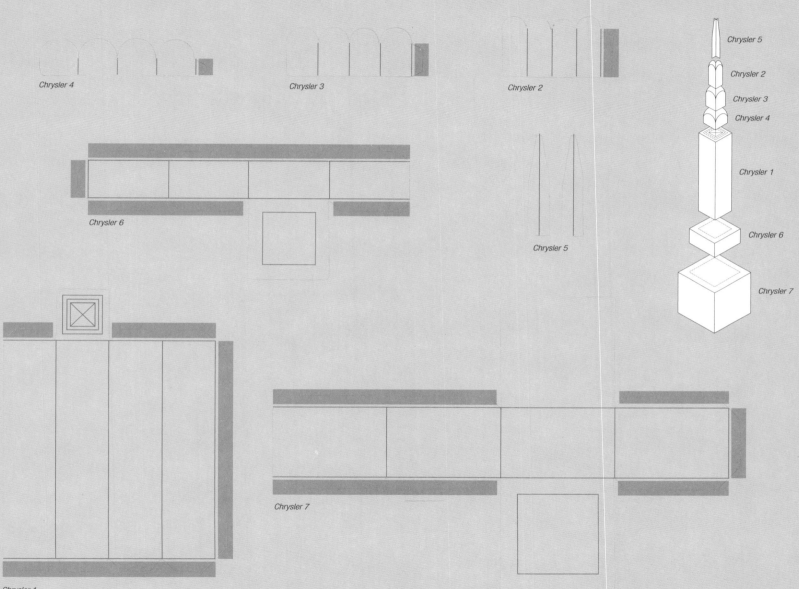

Chrysler 4

Chrysler 3

Chrysler 2

Chrysler 6

Chrysler 5

Chrysler 1

Chrysler 7

Chrysler 5
Chrysler 2
Chrysler 3
Chrysler 4
Chrysler 1
Chrysler 6
Chrysler 7

Brooklyn Bridge

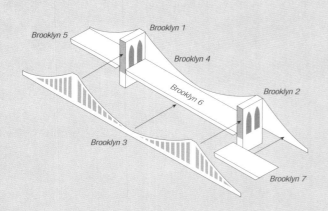

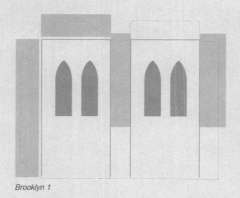

Brooklyn 1

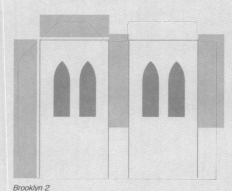

Brooklyn 2

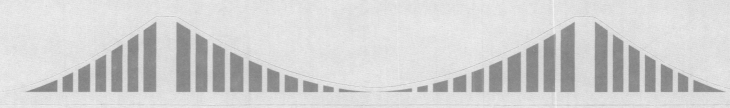

Brooklyn 3

Brooklyn 5

Brooklyn 6

Brooklyn 7

Brooklyn 4

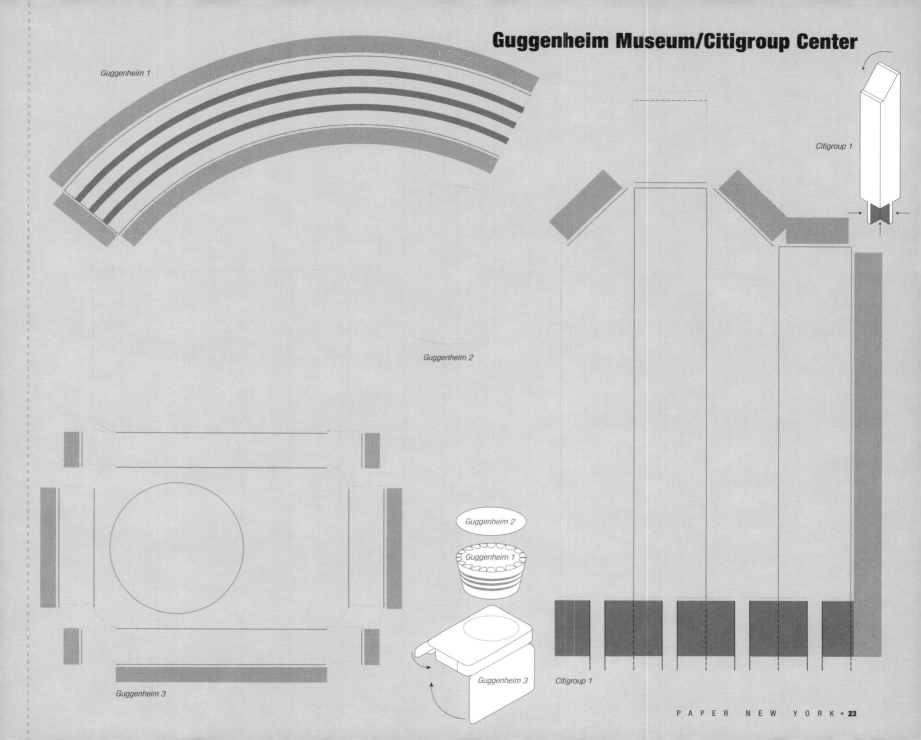

Guggenheim Museum/Citigroup Center

Guggenheim 1

Citigroup 1

Guggenheim 2

Guggenheim 3

Guggenheim 2

Guggenheim 1

Guggenheim 3

Citigroup 1

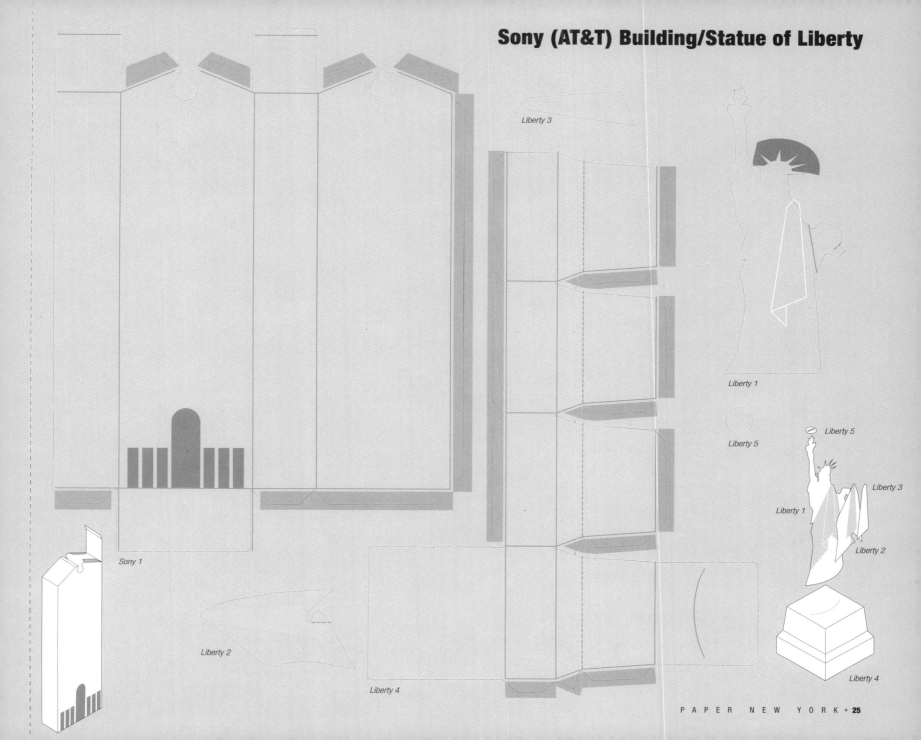

Liberty 3

Liberty 1

Sony 1

Liberty 5

Liberty 5

Liberty 3

Liberty 1

Liberty 2

Liberty 2

Liberty 4

Liberty 4

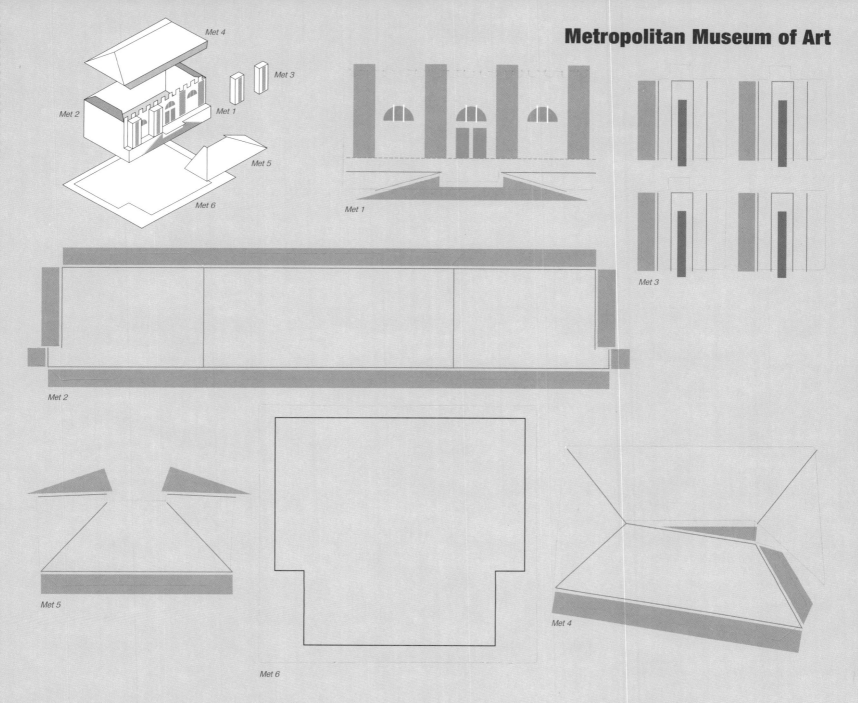

Metropolitan Museum of Art

Met 4

Met 3

Met 1

Met 2

Met 5

Met 6

Met 1

Met 3

Met 2

Met 5

Met 6

Met 4

Flatiron Building

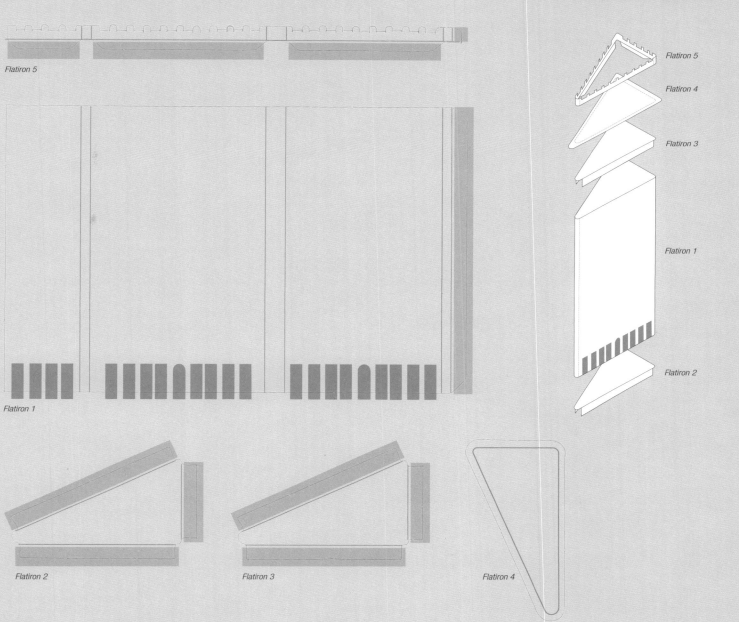

Flatiron 5

Flatiron 5

Flatiron 4

Flatiron 3

Flatiron 1

Flatiron 1

Flatiron 2

Flatiron 2

Flatiron 3

Flatiron 4

Subway 2

Subway 1

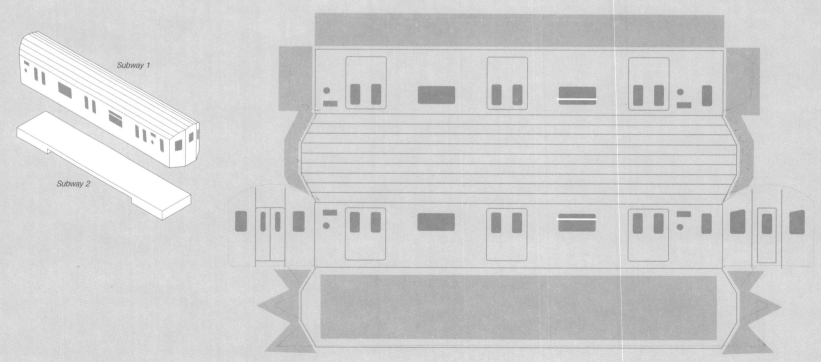

Subway 2

Subway 1

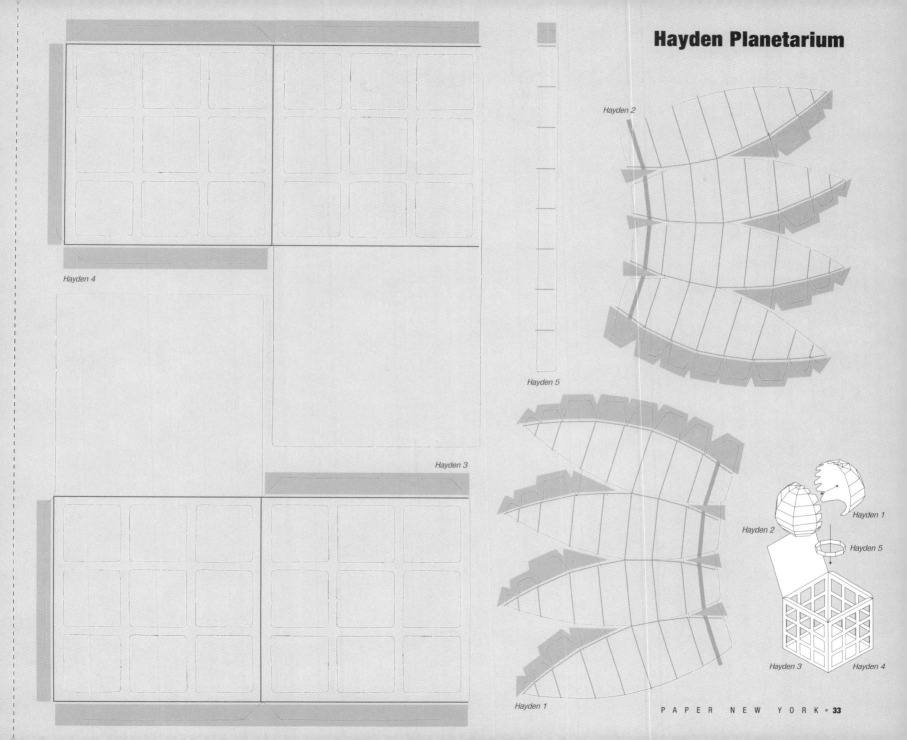

Hayden Planetarium

Hayden 2

Hayden 5

Hayden 4

Hayden 3

Hayden 2

Hayden 1

Hayden 5

Hayden 1

Hayden 3

Hayden 4

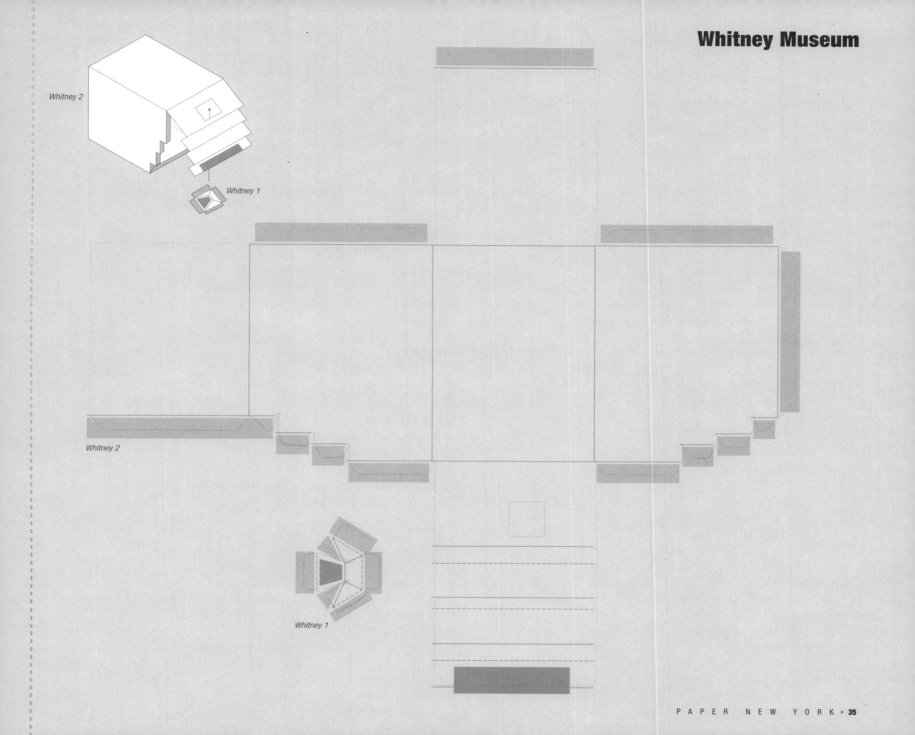

Whitney Museum

Whitney 2

Whitney 1

Whitney 2

Whitney 1

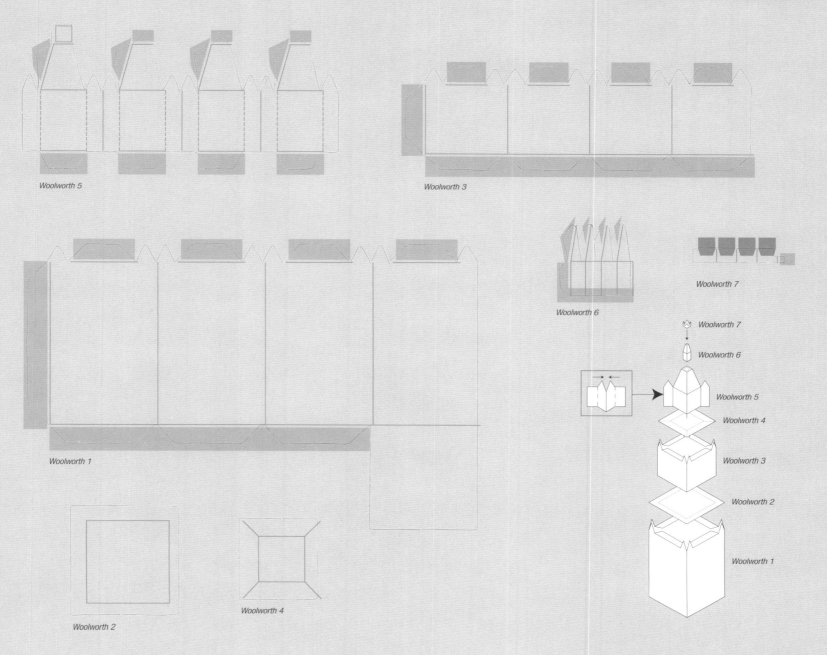

Woolworth 5

Woolworth 3

Woolworth 6

Woolworth 7

Woolworth 7

Woolworth 6

Woolworth 5

Woolworth 4

Woolworth 3

Woolworth 2

Woolworth 1

Woolworth 1

Woolworth 2

Woolworth 4

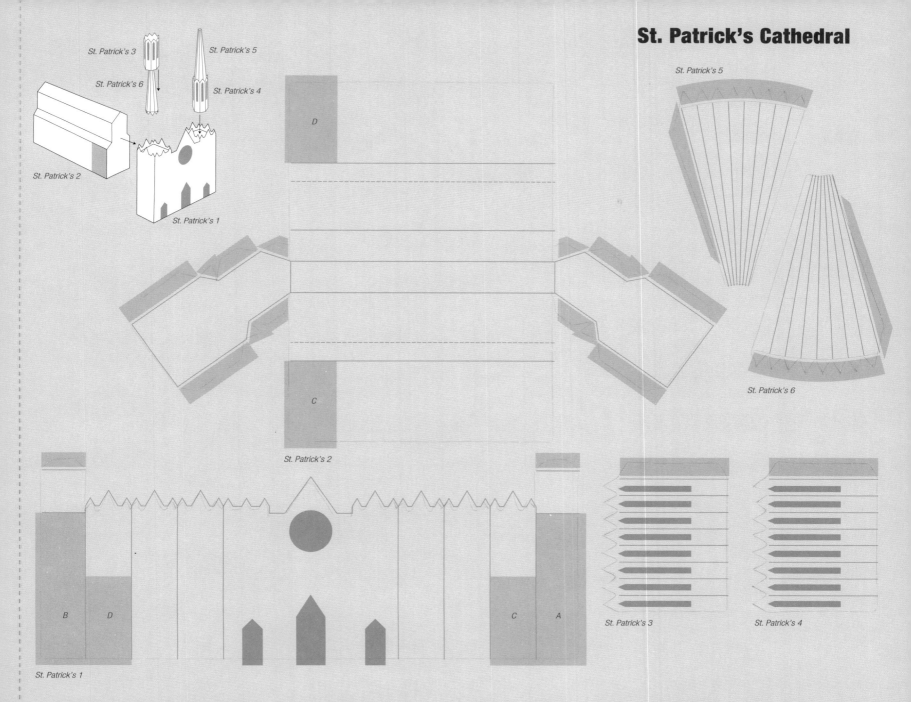

St. Patrick's 3

St. Patrick's 5

St. Patrick's 6

St. Patrick's 4

St. Patrick's 2

St. Patrick's 1

St. Patrick's 5

D

C

St. Patrick's 6

St. Patrick's 2

B   D

C   A

St. Patrick's 1

St. Patrick's 3

St. Patrick's 4

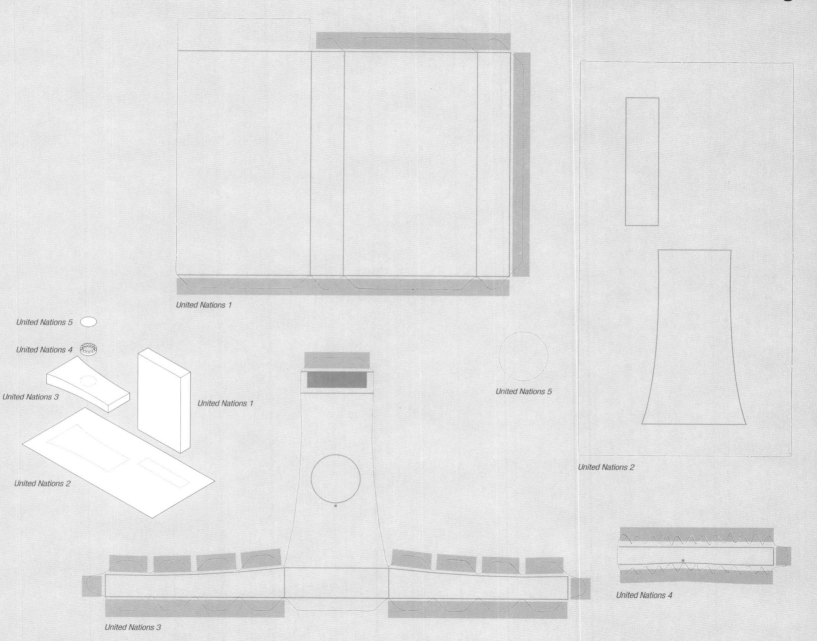

United Nations 1

United Nations 5

United Nations 4

United Nations 3

United Nations 1

United Nations 2

United Nations 5

United Nations 2

United Nations 3

United Nations 4

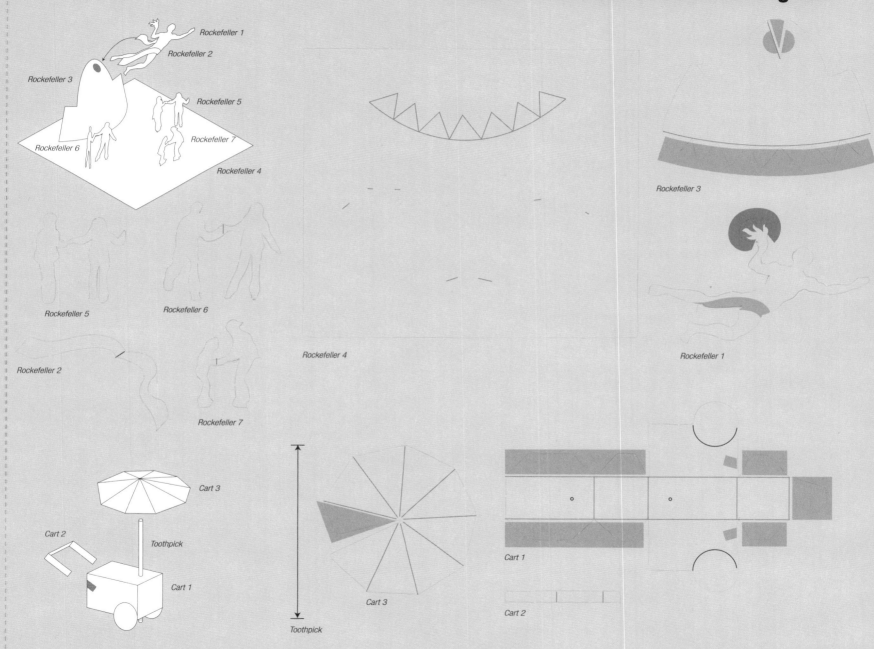

Rockefeller 1

Rockefeller 2

Rockefeller 3

Rockefeller 5

Rockefeller 6

Rockefeller 7

Rockefeller 4

Rockefeller 3

Rockefeller 5

Rockefeller 6

Rockefeller 2

Rockefeller 4

Rockefeller 7

Rockefeller 1

Cart 3

Cart 2

Toothpick

Cart 1

Cart 3

Toothpick

Cart 1

Cart 2

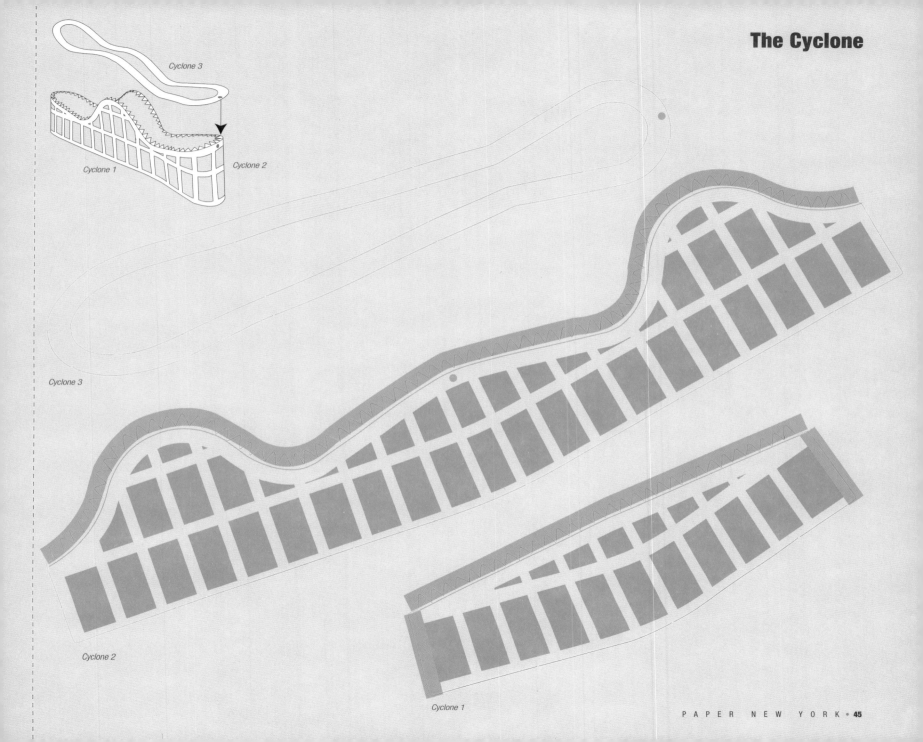

The Cyclone

Cyclone 3

Cyclone 1

Cyclone 2

Cyclone 3

Cyclone 2

Cyclone 1

Carriage 2

Carriage 1

Carriage 3

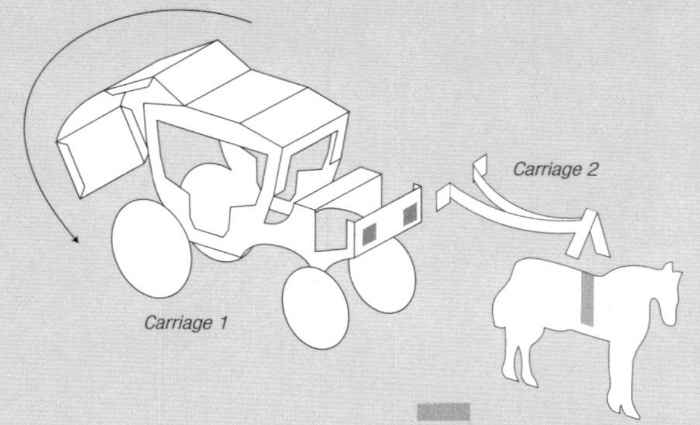

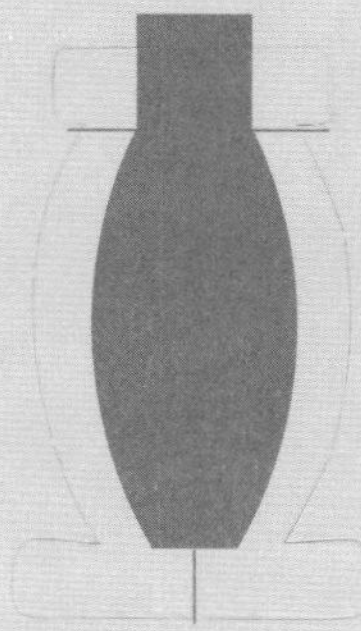

Carriage 2

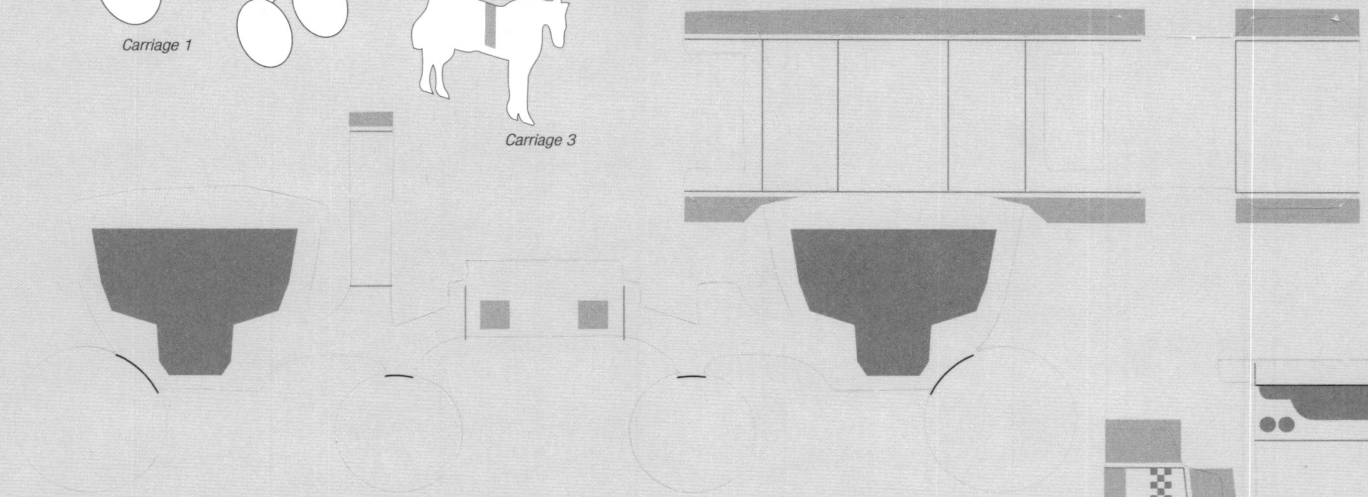

Carriage 1

Carriage 3

Cab 2

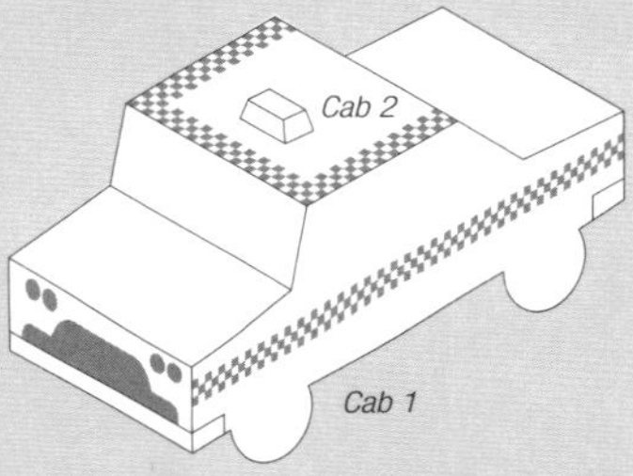

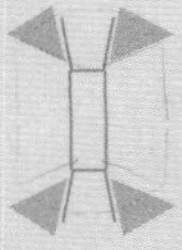

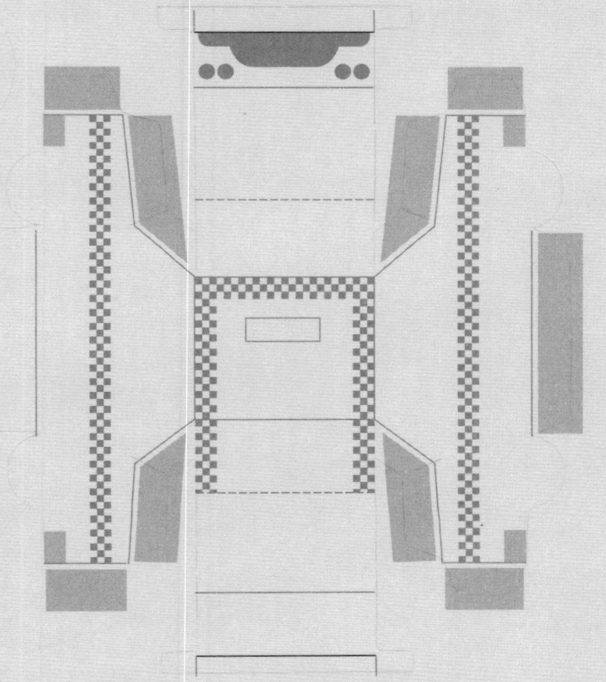

Cab 2

Cab 1

Cab 1